Sophie's Log

Thoughts and feelings in poetry and prose

How can the End
Be the Beginning Again
When All seems Lost?

Sophie Large

Written and illustrated by Sophie Large

Edited by
Cherry Large

Foreword by
Dame Judi Dench

All proceeds to
SOPHIE'S SILVER LINING FUND

ISBN 0 9534901 0 6

First Published 1998 by
SOPHIE'S SILVER LINING FUND
Registered Charity No. 1071883.
17, Silver Street, Chacombe, Banbury,
Oxon OX17 2JR, England.

Reprinted June 1999.
Reprinted July 2000.

Designed by Rosy Burke Design Associates Ltd.
19 Banbury Road, Chacombe, Banbury, Oxon OX17 2JN.

Printed in Great Britain by
Cheney & Sons Ltd,
Beaumont Road, Banbury, Oxon OX16 7RH.

Copies of this book can be obtained by post at a cost of £7.00 per book (to include P&P)
by sending a cheque made out to "Sophie's Silver Lining Fund" to the Fund's address above.

Detailed information about the Fund and its activities can be found
by visiting the Charity's Website at **www.silverlining.org.uk**

For all Sophie's
delightful friends

ACKNOWLEDGEMENTS

We are grateful to so many people who have encouraged us to produce this book, including Sally Foord-Kelcey, who conceived the idea of 'Sophie's Log', Lizzie Cotton, who typed such reams of Sophie's writing, David Pope and other kind people who read drafts and offered their advice, Rosy Burke, whose flair and expertise was so essential and who made it such fun, Shaun Mullins and Phil Ramm for their Photoshop artistry and Joyce Smith and many other teachers and mentors who encouraged Sophie to write her poetry and express herself in writing, drama and singing.

CONTENTS

FOREWORD
by Dame Judi Dench

Although I never knew Sophie, I didn't hesitate when Stephen and Cherry Large asked me to be patron of Sophie's Silver Lining Fund. I was so moved by the tragedy that ended Sophie's young life that I wanted to do what I could to help.

Sophie's Silver Lining Fund has been set up to help gifted and determined young actors and singers, and this book will help to raise funds. This collection of Sophie's work is just one aspect of her wide range of talents.

I urge you to support Sophie's Silver Lining Fund so that something positive can come out of the sad loss of such a unique young woman.

Judi Dench.

Street café in Hesdin, near Calais, France

INTRODUCTION

This book is a tribute to our beloved daughter Sophie, who died in a road accident when she was nineteen. She was an unusually smiley person with a powerful imagination, who gave love and joy to many people of all ages. She went straight into friendships in an uninhibited way and though she might occasionally suffer hurt as a consequence, she never let it get her down. Vibrant and sensitive, she shared her life openly and generously with all. Like any teenager, she could easily get cross or upset, but she was never resentful and a slammed door would inevitably open a few moments later with a smile and a conciliatory word.

Sophie's younger brother, Oliver, unable to sleep the night after she died, spent time in her bedroom and came upon some notebooks of her writing, all neatly filed in a bookcase. One of these notebooks was entitled The Log. He was astounded at the imaginative, compelling and inspiring nature of this particular notebook and the next morning drew our attention to it. He told us that he had found much food for thought and personal happiness within its contents. It had been used as a log when Sophie had been a passenger on a children's educational cruise in the Eastern Mediterranean when aged about fourteen. She seems to have returned to this particular notebook regularly in the succeeding years, and many thoughtful essays and holiday diaries, notes, lists for real and imaginary expeditions, drafts of poems and so on are found there. We have arranged this book in a similar style.

We found another beautifully illustrated notebook which contained finished versions of her own poems. We refer to it in the text as her Best Poetry book.

Sophie's Log contains all of Sophie's poems and a medley of her other writings extracted from numerous notebooks, diaries and letters. We have divided the book into three chapters, entitled Childhood, containing work written when she was nine to thirteen, Growing up, thirteen to sixteen, and Maturing, sixteen to nineteen.

Sophie's writings form a wonderful archive of her life and work and naturally they are a great source of comfort to those of us who were close to her. We hope the reader will enjoy Sophie's Log and find it interesting and perhaps inspiring.

CHERRY AND STEPHEN LARGE
Sophie's parents

This book

This book within doth stories tell,
Of fairies, witches, Hea'n and Hell,
Read on, my friend, enjoy my book,
I prithee now to take a look.

God bless you, Sir, Madame, Miss,
Which ever title bring you bliss,
enjoy these stories, when they're writ,
'Till Then you'll have to wait a bit.

     by Sophia C.A. Large

Found written in the front of a notebook that Sophie had just received as a Christmas present, aged fifteen. Her full name was Sophia Caroline Addams Large.

~

~This book within doth stories tell, ~
~ Of fairies witches, Hea'n and Hell, ~
~ Read on, my friend, enjoy my book, ~
~ I prithee now to take a look. ~

~ God bless you, sir, madame, miss, ~
~ Which ever title bring you bliss, ~
~ enjoy these stories, when they're writ, ~
~ 'Till Then you'll have to wait a bit. ~

~

BY SOPHIA C. A. LARGE

In the Childhood chapter we have selected poems and writings from Sophie's earliest notebooks. We have deliberately left her mispellings in place, copying the pieces exactly as we have found them. Some of the poems have been subsequently worked on and improved by Sophie, especially those she chose for a Poetry Society examination where the candidates were required to recite their own poetry. These were written out in her Best Poetry book.

Sophie's home life was spent in lovely rural surroundings. When she was twelve she went to boarding school, St. Swithun's School in Winchester. Her two brothers went to Winchester College. We think she must have found writing letters, poems and diaries a real comfort to her when she was lonely or a bit homesick.

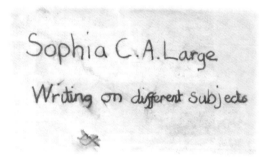

Chapter One

Childhood

My ten wishes

Helpful wishes

1. No more wars.
2. Pollution to disappear.
3. To make it impossible to pollute in any way.
4. For the weather to behave itself, so
   Spring. Fresh, sunny, rainy, clear.
   Summer. Sunny, hot, rain enough for agricultural uses only at night.
   Winter. Cold, snowy, no rain, just snow, clear skys when not snowing.
   Autumn. Mainly dry, raining sometimes.
5. For the ground to become furtile in non-furtile countries.

My personel wishes

6. My dad to be sent one million pounds.
7. To be able to talk to animals.
8. To be able to breath under water.
9. To be able to ride really well.
10. To be able to fly when I want.
11. To be able to become small wenever required.

Aged ten.

Sophie had added a covering note to this asking that it should not be shown to her Dad. We are not sure why!

Leaving the nest

Why, Oh Why did I leave home?
All that happened wen I left,
Is I have to fend for myself,
Instead, my plump worms, (given by her)
Turn into old caterpillers (got by me)
Instead of a warm nest I have an old pach of leaves
(or Just my Wing)
So Why, Oh Why did I leave home?
Ever since I left the nest,
I have not seen my brothers or father and mother,
Once or twice I have been almost caught by a cat,
I feel unsafe and frightened,
Since I am not a good flyer yet,
(Nor are my brothers, I sopose)
And how I miss the feathers on mum's backside,
But, after all this, I keep my mum's word of advise,
That I must never get worried or frightened
When in danger because if you panick you will get
Caught, killed, or ingered.

By Robert Robin.

By Sophie Large

*One of Sophie's earliest poems,
written when aged about ten.*

15

All over the world

All over the world animals and birds have been killed by poison, oil, waste, our own machines and lots more.

We kill animals and birds for there meat, fur and feathers. We kill hundreds of tipes of birds with oil and waste throwne into the sea. In places people will shoot animals for fun, such as hares, foxes and rabbits.

In places we cut down birds homes and fill in worans, sets, and any other animals that live under ground.

Forist fires are another danger too wildlife. Some people say they have seen animals walking out of forist fire with there coats on fire burning to death.

Swans are being poisened by lead. Otters are being hunted for playing when they kill fish and leave them rotting. Now they and lots like them are rare.

BY SOPHIA C. A. LARGE

When Sophie was nine she wrote several book reviews and short pieces about music and things that interested her in a new notebook she had just received for Christmas.

Book reviews

The Flower Fairy Poems by Cicely Barker

These stories were brought to my attention by the mystery magic in them. Some people can see this magic. It is a beautiful book, and the Charictors are amusing, sweet misterious and shy.

The poems are read all over England and are very popular with little girls. What's more now there are flower fairy dolls which are also very attractive. Though I don't know Cicely Barker, I am shore she is a mysterious, fun person with a good imagination and I am shore that all of those who are luky enough to know her think how much loved she must be!

S.C.A Large, January the 26th 1988

Black Beauty by Anna Sewell

In this story Anna Sewell has given people a good idea of what a horse has to be sensitive about.

This story could almost have been true and like Glyn Fewer* has a good description of things, though in a different sort of way. Her book is not quite an easy book, but is good for the education of reading for moderate-aged children.

Once again imagination was put in by how animals talk, but then I suppose they might talk.

The basik story is the life of a horse. A very luky horse. Her Book is a bit like advice, and I should advice any rider who has just started to learn to ride to read this book, before they start learning.

Sophie C.A. Large, January the 26th 1988.

Aged nine.

Author of Bryn of Brockle Hanger.

Music reviews

Airs and dances by Respighi

I like this music because it has a way of changing from loud, exciting music to soft, comforting music.

It makes me spellbound, and I think I could sit for hours listening too it and looking into the fire on a cold winter night. One can picture the music in their imagination. It gives me a happy comfortable peaceful feeling when soft, and a sort of exciting feeling when loud.

Sometimes I see a fair ground of happy children. Sometimes I see people in the 16th century danceing, sometimes little birds hopping around. Once even I saw a garden with a lovely lady sitting under a tree playing the flute. All of these were in my imagination.

Patchel Bel Canon

This piece of music reminds me of a funeral my mother and father went to. It makes a small lump come to my throat. It is sad and flowing, and it could be pictures of a late person. Or it could be of people having a wonderful time in a wild, open place, or of love in the winter snug in a warm cottage with a fire burning merrily. What ever it is, it is a touching piece of music, which goes straight to the heart.

Aged nine.

Catkins

Catkins, hanging in the sun,
Pollen enough for everyone,
Will you still hang there when I'm gone,
When your job is done?

I wish I were like you, small and light,
When I die I think I might
Soar and fly through the night,
'Till my job is done.

Drip

Drip, drip, drip!
I turn.
Drip, drip, drip!
A tap is running.
Drip, drip, drip!
I walk over.
Drip, drip, drip!
Squeeeik!
Drip!
It stops.

These two poems were written out in Sophie's Best Poetry book and may have been improved by her in later years.

Traditions

WINTER – New Year's Day

Allelullia To Our God
For Bringing in another Year,
New, untarnished
Squeaky clean,
May it be a good one
May it be a good one.

SPRING – Easter Day

Easter Egg hunt

A silver glass of water.
Each puts a tear of water to their
eye, youngest to oldest.
I cry for the pain You suffered
And I thank You for loving me
(Before Breakfast)

SUMMER – Midsummer's Day

Evening
(I dunno. Mebe I'll think properly when
I have kids or nephews and neices or school children.)
Oh, my God!

AUTUMN – A fine Autumn day

Go for a walk in a beech wood & catch 12 leaves
& put them in your boot. 12 leaves for 12 lucky months of the year.

Jimmy Quick

Jump for Joy!
Oh, jump for joy!
I'm riding Jimmy today!
This pony of mine
Is quite sublime,
Lively, frisky and gay.

He jumps with a spring,
He'll eat anything,
Especially tangerine peels,
He'll gallop away,
All through the day,
As if the devil were at his heels.

His friendly eye
Is full up high
With merry, yet willful glee,
If you're tossed to the ground,
He'll soon be found,
Anxiously nuzzling your knee.

Another poem from Sophie's Best Poetry book.

What I would need

to go on an exploration journey – for a day

Tent	water bottle
Sleeping bag	kettle
	packet of tea
compass	half loaf of bread
map	cheese
log book	2 tins of tuna
pencil case	2 tins of baked beans
herbal book	butter
telescope	packet of potatoes
waterproof	tin plate
jersey	tin mug
	knife, fork spoon

Sophie seems to have forgotten a tin opener !
She was a great list maker, both for real and imaginary events.
Her notebooks and diaries are full of them.

The moonlight horse

I tossed and turned in my bed until I think I dozed, then I woke – I don't know why, to find my room was flooded with silver light. I got out of bed and went to the window. There were funny lights everywhere that flitted about, up and down, in the silver sky. Then a shape appeared over the horizon from the silvery moon, a horse – yes, a horse it was, with silver wings. I promise it, I am not fibbing, it was a horse. It came over to my room and I climbed on his back. We sawed threw the air. Every now and then he glanced at the moon his home. I think it was a dream but no – my legs are covered in moon dust. Will they believe me? No! Think again!

The pleasant scents of spring

When I was very, very small,
I swung upon a swing,
And slid quick down the old stone wall
In the pleasant scents of spring.

When I was relatively small
I succeeded, with a sling
That got me onto the trapeze tall,
In the pleasant scents of spring.

When I was younger, six and all,
I loved the great old field
Where horses graze until the call
Of the pleasant scents of spring.

And now I'm older, ten and all,
I long for trapeze and swing,
And the old stone wall, and the field of green,
In the pleasant scents of spring.

From Sophie's Best Poetry book.

The stream and the tree

Seasons pass as the stream runs on, old and unfeeling, unknowing to all around it. It never began, it will never naturally end. It doesn't care if it rains or snows, so long as it gets to its destination. It runs past a little sapling, not that it looks, it doesn't mind. The winter snows sear the tree, leaving it a little bent, a little wiser. And yet, the stream doesn't care if it rains or snows, it flows on.

The spring comes and brings the tree to life. It freshens it, and cleanses it. On the stream ambles, unfeeling. The little tree feels the spring, and grows as fast as it can, before the summer comes, which it does, bringing heat, insects, and dust. The little tree wilts and sighs. If only it could sit down! Still the stream passes, unheeding of the tree or nature – if a little thinner. But rain or no, on it travels.

At last, Autumn comes, bringing a release of rain and winds. The little tree is tired. It is time to sleep. And as it sleeps, its leaves fall. The stream never rests, it flows on despite the cold, gaining speed and water as it goes. It surges forward, and looks almost happy – but this is an illusion. It feels nothing, sees nothing. Its only care is to get to the sea . . . to the sea . . .
Then suddenly a terrible thing happens. It is stopped by a dam, and has its only wish taken away from it – the wish to get to the sea . . . , and it turns into a useless wetness for you and me to drink.

A way up a mountain, an old oak tree stands. Many seasons have passed leaving it a little bent, a little wiser. The stream has gone, but a huge reservoir is to be seen in the valley green.

The End

Catastrophically speaking

"Catastrophically speaking"
The teacher implied,
The dining room was filthy,
When he went inside:
The wine was on the sideboard,
Seeping through the meat,
The plates were smashed all over –
The bits stuck in your feet!

"Catastrophically speaking,"
(The man began to shout,)
The garden was quite hopeless,
When they all went out,
The flowerbed was awful,
Earth on the tangled lawn
"It really was a pity",
The cook began to mourn.

"Catastrophically speaking",
The teacher said,
The room was in a shambles
When he went to bed.
The sheets were topsy-turvey
The ink began to spill
Upon the spotless bedmat –
The stain is on there still!

"Catastrophically Speaking",
The teacher sneered,
The Master looked a nervous wreck
When he reappeared.
His house was quite demolished,
His horse was running wild,
His face had gone bright yellow
And he wimpered like a child,

Catastrophically speaking,
A monkey got loose in the house!

From Sophie's Best Poetry book.

Beneath the bracken

Beneath the bracken
By the stream
Lives a pixie
Decked in green.
His wings are clear
As clear can be,
But none can see him,
Only me.

Beside the oak tree,
In the roots,
Lives an elf
With mouse-skin boots.
He plays the pipe
Just like a bird,
By me alone
His song is heard.

'Neath the rose bush,
Blooming wild,
Is a lovely fairy child.
The fragrance of the bush
Is she,
But no one knows this,
Only me.

Within the waters
Of the brook,
Lives a water nymph
In a nook.
'Tis she that makes
The water shine,
But this knowledge
Is only mine.

These things are seen
Alone by me,
Because most people
Foolish be.
For see, smell, taste, touch,
Hear, they will,
But all beyond
For them bodes ill.

And so, my children,
Hear my tale,
The gift of magic
Will prevail
Within your minds,
You alone can see
The elf who lives
Beneath the tree.

From Sophie's Best Poetry book.

Dearest Parents

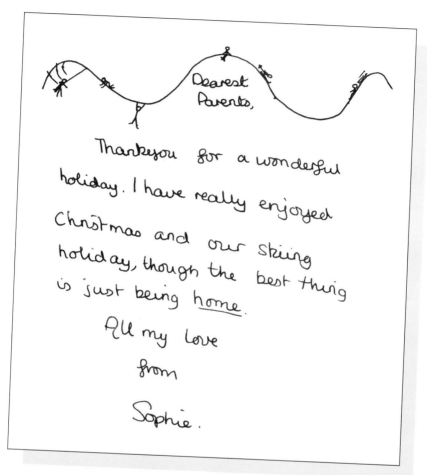

> Dearest Parents,
>
> Thankyou for a wonderful holiday. I have really enjoyed Christmas and our skiing holiday, though the best thing is just being <u>home</u>.
>
> All my love
>
> from
>
> Sophie.

A Haiku

This is a haiku, or short poem with a deep meaning.

How can the End
Be the Beginning again
When All seems Lost?

Don't read on for a minute, I'll tell you what it means on the next page –

Have you thought about it?

Because if you haven't, don't read on.

It means that when something dreadful happens, like someone dies, it seems the end, and yet it is the beginning of coping without. See?

Looking forward to seeing you,

love Sophie

x x x x

This is taken from a letter sent to her grandparents in Scotland; at the time her grandfather was seriously ill.

Tomas' home

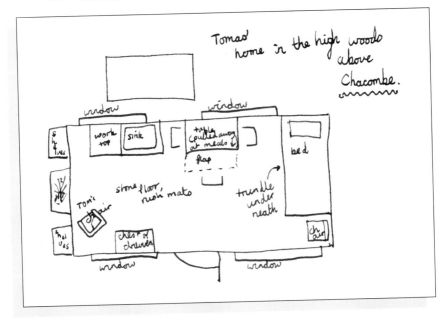

An old derelict shepherd's hut intrigued Sophie.

To Grandmother

A bright light all around me,
And a deep happiness filling me.
I laugh, I jump, I sing, I shout for joy.
For this is a joyous place, and God is with me.

Calm, still lake of water, all still and like glass.
The sun peeps over the hills, and a brilliant light
Shines over the water to me, laughing for joy.
For this is a joyous place, and God is with me.

Waving green grass, on a hill,
I lie in it and think, looking in to the blue sky.
Joy is all around me, and time flies.
For, Grandmother, this is a joyous place, and God is with me.

Time, here, is like nothing on earth,
And I am soon with my loved ones.
I am happy, free, and clothed in white.
For this is a joyous place and God is with me.
Happy, Forever and Ever,

Amen.

Sophie was twelve when she wrote this poem, shortly after Grandfather died.

Take me, O Lord

Take me, O Lord, for the snow are calling o'er,
Take me to the happy land of love and light.

Take me, Dear Lord, for the wind is getting stronger,
Take me to the Paradise unknown to our eyes.

Take me, Dear Lord, for the sun is swiftly setting,
Take me to the place eternal, love and light.

Take me, Dear Lord, for my eyes are getting heavy,
Take me to my resting place, to Heaven.

This is a song Sophie wrote for a friend whose mother had recently died – it has a very haunting and lovely melody which she also composed. We have a very precious recording of Sophie aged just twelve singing it.

Swans on the Wing

There is nothing so simple
Or so grave, or so gentle,
Or powerful and graceful
As swans on the wing.

There is nothing as graceful
Serene or as stately
Or wistful or mournful
As swans on the wing.

There is little as peaceful
As watching them gliding
On wings over water,
All ruffled by wind.

All praise be to flying,
So with likeness to dying,
Flying so gracefully
Far and away.

Goothrans

Goothrans, the Island of Dreams and Expectations

Many, many years ago, long before I was born, or you, when the Island of Goothrans was inhabited by animals alone, a very insignificant thing happened. A boat popped up on the horizon, way to the North, and saw the island. Then, the boat left. After that, the People came. There are only ever twelve People, they live for ever, because those People had been sent to explore this uncharted island, and they had decided to stay.

Goothrans is the Island of Dreams and Expectations – so if you ever landed there, would you want to leave?

And those twelve people were these. Mary of the Bow, David of the Lance, Marcus of the Waters, Lorna of the Land, Elizabeth of the Animals, Sophia of the Birds, Petro of the Fish, Rosemary of the Plants, Simon (Sion) of the Wind, Philip of the Rain, and the two highest of the Twelve, Fynn of the Dark and Anne of the Light.

Of course, those weren't their names when they set out from their port in the boat in search of the strange land. They all had surnames like Jones and Smith. And they all worked like normal men.

But when they reached the Island, they changed. Not immediately – the process was very slow, but it happened.

Their boat was called the Ariadne, and she was a beautiful vessel, with full sails of blue and plain wooden sides. The expedition was lead by Anne and Fynn. They were the oldest, being around twenty five. The youngest was Elizabeth who was just eight, and very proud of it. Her job was lookout, which she took very seriously, and sat on the prow, her legs dangling down. It was she who first saw Goothrans. She shouted, "Land! Land!" and the captain Fynn saw it, and all the crew saw it.

They landed on the beach and Lorna set up camp. Scouting parties were set up. David and Mary, together with Sophia and Elizabeth the two youngest, went south to the edge of the woods before coming back again. Petro had caught some fish, and Rosemary had found a patch of wild garlick. They had their first meal together on the lovely Island of Goothrans as the sun sank, and they prepared for sleep.

Sophie drew many charts of her imaginary island.

Over the next moon they found many things. They saw the mountain to the North and found the lake with a river flowing from it. The wood or forest, they discovered, was dark and hostile – although Rosemary seemed unafraid of it and Elizabeth as well seemed to like it even.

The people in them had started to develop. Petro caught fish and swam frequently. He had somehow grown taller and thinner – with the Grace of fishes already upon him. Rosemary could find any herbs and make anything grow. She became brown from the sun and a little stooped, as time went on, and her hair grew wild, like branches of trees. Elizabeth changed little, her eyes sparkled more and was able to approach animals in a way no-one else could. Mary had fashioned a bow for herself. She never missed. David as well was deadly with the Lance. Lorna seemed shorter, plumper and knew exactly where plants would best grow and where a fire would light best. Simon seemed aloof, wild-haired and always on the go. Philip knew when it would rain. He seemed thinner, and more wiry. He and Simon were great friends, along with Petro.

But the two who changed the most were Anne and Fynn, for they had been Graced with the most terrible and wonderful gifts. Fynn became more compact and serious. He had jet black hair and an eagle nose, and looked more and more like his Power. Anne became sweet, Graceful, full of love and carefree joy. She and Fynn did not get on very well.

To start with, the people remained as one body, travelling around the Island. No-one understood the changes of the others, or realized the change in themselves.

They may have been the People of the Island, but they were human too, and their powers often caused disagreements. Whenever they shot food, Elizabeth would cry and scream. She and Rosemary stayed together, as did Mary and David. Sophia and Petro were closely linked, both had a way with fish and birds. Sophia had a birdlike quality – with little eyes, peaky, small body and a tendency to move in a jerky motion. She too had a disliking for the warriors, and gradually Petro refused to catch any more fish. The Weather People tended to roam a lot together, often as much as two days from the main body. But as it will happen, they drifted apart. The land of Goothrans became separated, in a way worse than boundaries. Petro could be found on the coast, Sophia on the mountains and Elizabeth and Rosemary in the woods. Fynn, heavily burdened by his gift, lived in the heart of the woods, in the hollow of a great pine tree, right near the middle. Anne would be found anywhere but the woods, flitting around as the fancy took her, in love with her surroundings. Philip and Simon separated, Philip to the plains, and Simon to the Hills. In their own ways, they grew and matured into their gifts, looking the same but very different from normal Humans – had a normal human seen one, they would have seen the difference.

The rest of the story hasn't been yet, the future can be seen by no one, but somehow, through the mists of time, all will come right, and Goothrans shall live in Peace, the Gifts given by the elements of life will once more combine.

How do you think it will happen?

We think Sophie was about thirteen when she wrote this.

Sophie had much to write about in this period of her life. She had become painfully aware that she was a bit of an outsider, an 'uncool' person. She was academically able. She was developing her singing and drama skills both in school and outside. She joined the National Youth Music Theatre and later, to her enormous delight, was accepted by the National Youth Theatre.

She maintained many friendships by letter-writing. Some of her diary entries were addressed to an imaginary friend she called Arion. We have since discovered that there was a Greek poet and musician of this name who flourished about B.C. 700. According to legend, he was cast into the sea by mariners, but carried to safety on the back of a dolphin. We can only speculate that Sophie was aware of him, but he seems to us to be a highly likely choice of confidante!

She reflected much about illness and dying and bereavement, experiencing the passing of both of her grandfathers and her beloved elderly friend 'Aunty' Eva.

She spent many happy family holidays in Scotland and Ireland. Some holidays were spent in Europe, camping and touring. She joined a children's educational cruise in the Eastern Mediterranean. She went on two flotilla sailing holidays in Turkey. She went on several riding holidays. After her GCSE examinations she went with her School Senior Choir to sing in churches and cathedrals in Florence and Venice. She went twice to the Edinburgh Festival, and was very inspired by the fringe theatre productions she saw there. She adored the three week introductory course of drama workshops for new members of the National Youth Theatre.

Chapter Two

Growing up

My Johnnie of Scotland

My Johnnie is a gypsy,
Born on the slopes of Screel,
And there my darling liveth,
The mountain he doth feel.

He wears a leather doublet,
A cap with a pheasant's feather,
He shoots with a bow and arrow,
On his pony, he calls Heather.

And his laugh is of the springtime,
His hair curled like young fern,
His smile the sun of summer,
Up on the Scottish burn.

My heart is his forever,
But it breaks to think if I
Had gone to live with Johnnie,
Then I would surely die.

His spirit is as wild as roe-deer,
I could not bring him down
From up there on his mountain,
Into my country home.

So now we have been parted,
Our childhoods differ so.
I could not live on his mountain,
Nor he to my house could go.

Sophie regularly visited her grandparents' home in south west Scotland.

Annie's tale

The tide ebbed from the estuary,
Out past Hestan Island,
And the sun sank low behind Ben Gairn
When I saw Annie leave.
A fleeting glimpse and moment
So short and yet so long
And the tide ebbed out past Hestan
In the setting sun – yes
The tide ebbed out past Hestan
In the setting sun.

Her hair whipped out behind her
Like the reeds, rustling and moaning;
Her bare feet the very seabed that
She walked across, indifferent
To the seafowl
Calling long and sad.
And lonely – oh, so lonely,
Like the low and angry clouds,
Like the tide, cast out past Hestan,
Skulking low and swiftly o'er the mud flats,
And pushed by the wind.

Desolate and lonely, like the slopes of Screel,
Her shoulders hunched, abandoned by all.
I would have called her – for she turned.
Her eyes were wild and stormy,
Like the sea – so full of anger, hate,
And tears, lost and whipped away
By the wind. Her cheeks were tinged with red
From the setting sun o'er Gairn,
And she turned away,
Merging with the mourning tide.

The legend of "daft Ann" of Hestan Island, off the Solway coast, fascinated Sophie.

Israel

Extract from Sophie's cruise log – day four

Israel, as a country, was as much or even more than I had hoped. It is a beautiful, peaceful country. Our guide, who was a Jew herself, told us with great pride how they had improved and helped the country, planting trees in the desert, rebuilding towns, churches and universities.

"The desert will bloom" was the prophecy, and it has. We saw the nomads, still living as Abraham had lived. We went past Jericho, and through the wilderness of Judea. Then we went through the desert, and down past the Good Samaritan Inn. We are not visiting Bethlehem, and for that I am very sad. But I have my whole life ahead to do something about it.

Then we went below sea level, and down to the lowest place on earth, the Dead Sea. We swam in the Dead Sea. It was a very strange sensation, floating on the water. There wasn't anyone else there apart from our group. Surprise, surprise, there was a fun park there, where we got rid of the salt. I took of bottle full of water from the Dead Sea, and some palm leaves.

On the way back to Jerusalem, we stopped at the Jewish children's war memorial. Six million Jews were killed. One million were children. This was by far the most moving thing we ever did, more than the Church of the Holy Sepulchre. The memorial was in a cave. The walls were lined with mirrors. In the room were six candles, representing each million, and on the mirrors the lights reflected millions and millions of times. The lights went back into eternity, each light representing one of the lives lost. It made me very sad and very moved. It was lovely, terrible, scary, truthful and beautiful. I shall remember that for ever, the nameless millions who died because of what they were.

Jerusalem, I have to say I found somewhat disappointing, if that is the right word. We entered into the old town by the Dung Gate and into a kind of bazaar. The street vendors tried to flog us things. No-one pick-pocketed me, thankfully. You could hear the Muslim priests singing prayers in the minarettes, calling them to prayer, and it was interesting. The streets were narrow and crowded.

The Church of the Holy Sepulchre – well, I don't know. It's not for me to say, really, how I feel. It is different for everyone. But for me it was rather disappointing. It was terribly overdone, over-decorated and covered in gold, incense, myrhh and all the rest, bedecked with semiprecious stones and gold. Ugh! I should have preferred a simple chapel of plain stone, or a hill with a cross marking the place and a plaque. Anything but such a vast, pampered, over-decorated (and so on) place. Anyway, then we went to the Bazaar, where I bought my plain olive wood crosses and one decorated one for Grandmother.

And finally we went to the gardens of Gethsemane. The olive trees were huge, but the branches were too far away for me to pluck a branch for peace. Never mind. It was lovely, but I don't think it was like how Jesus knew it except for the trees. We also went to the Wailing Wall. I would have liked to have gone up and put in a word of prayer – but I didn't as it was rather embarrassing. There were many Jews praying, because this is the evening of the Passover. Then we came back.

I bought 4 crosses   £1
         1 poster   50p
         1 cross   £1

When Sophie was fourteen she went on a children's educational cruise in the Eastern Mediterranean.

All my life

All my life I walked in shadow
Of my mother's good and worth,
"Follow in your mother's footsteps"
Said the vicar at my birth.

I tried, I tried to match my mother,
But I failed when I began –
To follow in your mother's footsteps
That is easier said than done.

She was lovely, I was plain.
She smiled and laughed, I thought I should.
I could not follow in her footsteps –
But my sister could.

She came later; one year gone,
My mother loved her more each day.
She followed well in mother's footsteps,
I was left alone to play.

Some day I will match my sister,
And I'll match my mother, too.
I needn't follow in their footsteps –
I'll follow dad's, that's what I'll do.

This poem appeared in a St. Swithun's school magazine. Sophie in fact didn't have a sister.

The truth of the Welsh mountain ponies

A happy little pony once I saw,
While trekking across a mountain moor,
I fell in love with that little pony,
But what I saw was a lie, a phony.

In Spring the ponies thrive as all,
They're sleek and fat when comes the fall,
They multiply in strength and peace,
By summer, pangs of hunger cease.

Summer days are hot and long,
Insects attack them in a throng,
The water becomes less and less,
The grass dry, the stream a muddy mess.

And now, alas, Autumn is near,
The days are shorter, give no more cheer,
The beasts are lashed with wind and rain,
And wish the sun would come again.

And now winter is here once more,
The snow is deep, and will not thaw,
The food is almost gone, and yes!
The number of ponies is less.

And finally then comes the Spring,
There's food enough for everything,
But sadly the ponies' congregation
Will shortly be a shorter nation.

The dogs are hungry,
And money is wanted by men,
Soon they will round up the ponies again,
Some ponies come, but more ponies go,
And I wish all ponies died old, or of snow.

A happy little pony once I saw,
While trekking across the mountain moor.
A happy pony no more I see,
And a feeling of hatred for men like me.

A riding holiday on the Black Mountain in Wales made Sophie aware of the plight of the wild ponies there. From Sophie's Best Poetry book.

Dearest Grandmother

How are you? I'm feeling positively radiant this morning – but how can one possibly fail to feel so when each breath of freezing, fresh air is like heady wine and the whole silvery, icy world is so enticing, and the sky such a blue tit colour of blue? At long last we have got rid of the rain and had the first proper Autumn morning, you know, when the sunlight catches each and every leaf and turns it ruddy gold, and the grass is delicately tinted with frost, and the air is so fresh and exhilarating you feel you could just dance? It has been my custom that for the first frost of the season I walk in it barefoot before the sun can touch it! It makes you feel so alive, it's like magic! (You should try it.)

I can imagine White Loch on a morning like this: the beech trees in front of your house just touched with gold and the lake covered in mist is faintly glowing silver. The trees on the opposite bank are wreathed in this moony mist and the sky, pale, pale blue, sets off the whole scene, with silver grass, silver everything, and the Scottish air is like freezing white wine as you breathe it in . . .

Oh, dear, I've got carried away! I'm sorry, I didn't mean to go on like this, but you must admit that it is on mornings such as this that the fairies dance and unicorns delicately pick their way through the misty, sun-streaked forest, a morning like this when Peter Pan surely is real, dancing with glee as only he can at the beauty of the world, only on a morning like this when the water nymph dances to the dawn in her deep, glowing world of the lake, only on a day like this that every fibre in everything is filled with magic . . .

This is an extract from a letter to
Sophie's Grandmother in Scotland.

White Loch

44

A new school year

We're going back to school tomorrow. Strangely, I can't wait! It'll be such fun being a senior, etc.

Anyway, this holiday has been the turning point of my life, you could say. I have done so many new things. I got off with my first boy, but I wasn't impressed – he was a 'goldfish'. I smoked for the first time. I know I shouldn't, but my principles are that I'll never, ever buy my own cigarettes. There. I had my first hang over, got drunk for the first time. Need I say more? Term starts, God Bless it. Let's hope it's a good'n.

The thing I've learned through the book Tall, Thin, and Blonde* is that being a Martian isn't so bad. 'Martian' is a term for the people that don't fit in well. If you accept it and do exactly what you want to do and say what you want there's no problem. I mean, I do have some good friends, and others who are quite good friends. There's no-one (at present) who I really loathe. So what's the problem? I'm really very lucky. I get on much better with people older than me. They have much more interesting things to say than loads of the trendies in my year. So it doesn't matter. I shall read, say what I want, do whatever I want to do. And if I start getting jealous of the people who all walk to school together, well I must tell myself to stop being such a sheep.

I'm going to diet these next two weeks to try and lose some puppy fat round my middle! I must buy a body this weekend which should be no probs. So I'm going to do a chart marking whether I did what I was supposed to do.
(And of course I didn't . . .).

Diary entry when Sophie was very nearly fifteen.

* by Dyan Sheldon, published by Walker Books

I have found my God!

I have found my God! I went to the Family Church today, and it was there I found Him.

The first thing that struck me as I entered was the number of people that were there. Usually there're about fifteen to thirty people huddled in the pews, while the rather dull organ drones on. Here people were laughing and calling. And the room was high and full of light from two enormous windows. There was a form of altar, but it was ignored through most of the service.

Oh, Arion, the hymns of praise we sang! We sang so loudly, so joyously, so fully, dancing and clapping in the love of God that we felt in and among us, us a whole, a single being. I cried, Arion. For here people openly professed their love of God so other people heard. Instead of hiding away within themselves, they were calling and loving and singing praise.

It was not like the forced singing of everyday hymns, whose words have little meaning. It was singing of the joy God gave us, and we were so thankful, Arion. So grateful I could have burst with the overwhelming new feeling of the truth.

Some people came and read pieces from the Bible or told of events that had moved them during the week, and some had come to ask for the prayers for others.

One man said we all bore fruit, but that fruit was not for us to keep, it was for others to enjoy. We had to give it away. A girl said how God handed to us what we were meant to have, and it was not right to try and get at what was behind it just because it looks better – but to take up a friendship or gift or opportunity and not try to get what was not offered to us.

The preacher said how we find it difficult to understand when God 'prunes us', when he chops away our fruitful branches along with the dead and the bad, festering ones, and how it's hard to understand that; but God has a reason for everything that happens and if you look, you could see this. It was amazing.

The communion really meant something – it meant remembering Jesus's love and compassion for us, and there was a cup about the size of a thimble full of Ribena and a piece from a real loaf of bread. It was beautiful, Arion, and ten sincere people, as they handed you the bread, said 'bless you, forever" or something. I felt that I couldn't care what happened next – I had learned more from this service than anything else I have ever done.

Aged fifteen.
At boarding school, Sophie was allowed to attend Sunday morning services at any nearby church.

Innocence

Wide eyes are staring
Fascinated with what chubby hands do.
Lips in motion – Brrrr! Brrrr!
Round face engrossed
In the model cars around his legs.
Flyaway hair hides
A flushed interested forehead.
Unknown to him,
I hear his senseless childish gabbles,
Immersed as he is in his own game.
The cars crash placidly into one another,
Or get endlessly filled
With gallons upon gallons of petrol.
He does not see me
As he continues his game,
Stumpy legs crossed under him,
Thick set arms working busily.
Innocence and sincerity,
Childhood and naivety,
Bundled up into one:
A plump little two year old,
Playing with his beloved cars
For hours and hours on end.
Then, suddenly,
With a click and a flash
The sweet scene is ended.
Dark eyes turn in surprise,
Face crumples in doubt.
He stands up abruptly, warily,
And looks foolishly
At the jumble of cars about his feet.
A sincere, beautiful pastime,
Brought to an end forever.
Innocence crushed
In one, foolish moment.
Why?

From Sophie's Best Poetry book.

Springtime

Dearest Auntie Eva,

How are you? I hope you are feeling better, because it really wouldn't do, you know, you feeling ill at a time of year like this! If you have a little energy, go and sit in your chair where you can see out of the side window of your house in your little sitting room, and look outside, and I will describe to you the beauties around us in our separate but very close (in spirit) domains. The most incredible change has come over the land, you will see. The air smells of wet soil and bright, tender green shoots which have all sprouted and grown as fast as they can, as if time were running out, which of course it isn't. The trees are covered in trembling bright green leaves – especially look at the hawthorn, Auntie Eva! Isn't it stunning? And the ground of woodlands and wastelands is coming alive with beautiful green. And the blossom! On my walk up to school each morning, along the side of the road, are lots of back gardens full of green plants, daffodils (almost over), tulips, and blossom of pale fragrant white and pink. I picked up a fallen one today. It is like a miniature rose, but much more delicate and translucent, fragile, but outstandingly beautiful.

Sophie was saddened by her 'Auntie' Eva's increasing frailty. Eva was a retired school teacher who befriended her and her brothers while they were growing up. Sophie was extremely fond of Eva and ever fascinated by her stories of life in the 'olden days' in the next door village, Middleton Cheney.

Sophie wrote 'Accepting death' at the time when she knew Eva was dying.

Accepting death

When you know death is inevitable, half the battle is over. All things die, even those that seem always to have been there. I know my Auntie Eva will die, maybe very soon, but I also know this: my Auntie Eva is the kindest, most loved lady I have ever known – serene, intelligent, attentive, loving. She devoted her life to loving other people and if anyone goes to heaven, she will. I find great comfort in knowing that even when someone is not here anymore, they are still somewhere better, seeing people who they love again.

For my Auntie Eva is old, and tired, and even though I love her dearly, it is not my right to want to keep her here longer than her body can keep her. What is the use of her staying here in a stiff, crumbling body when she wants to be young again? That is the gift of heaven. The chance to be young again. A year or two ago, I wrote a little poem:

> How can the End
> Be the Beginning again
> When All seems Lost?

Since I wrote that I have thought about it often. For the more I think about it the more true it seems. Even in our blackest hour, there is always a chance to get better. When a loved one dies, it is not the 'end' – there is no such thing as the end. It is always the beginning of a new thing, a chance to improve all the time.

When my Auntie Eva dies, she will go somewhere – I know not where – and start afresh. She will never die, she will live. Even if she is not with us, she is happy somewhere, probably with her family again, all those brothers and her parents who have died. She will be filled with joy.

And hard though it seems, it is important for us to be filled with joy also. Because we all know that it is hard for a loved one in old age – they feel useless and helpless. To die is a release from the old body into a new and vigorous one – how can we be sad about that? I love my Auntie Eva and because I love her I know that I must let go. She will go whether I like it or not so I must let her go with a happy heart, knowing that she is well now – no cancer, no illnesses, no loss of hearing or words. She can fulfil all those things she wanted to fulfil in her last life. That makes me very happy. Of course, I am only human, and therefore being human I am selfish, I don't want to let her go.

But I am happier now, because she is going to be so much happier. There is no end to anything, only many beginnings to take up and work on. The proof of what I say is all around us. After all, even after winter snows, the leaf and flower always grows. Even after the end there is always a beginning – hope.

There is always hope.

Imagination

My makeshift raft sits sluggishly in the stream.
The ferry stands, glittering in the sun . . .
Its cabin windows a thousand eyes . . .
(well, my doll had two eyes anyway.)
The porter helps a millionaire lift her luggage . . .
(my plastic lunch box makes the raft tilt so I remove it.)
The cars, buses and lorries enter the great ship's hold . . .
(pity my tricycle's too heavy.)
The great chains, holding it to anchor, slowly unwind . . .
(the bit of string attached to the raft and
a stone breaks, but the raft is still.)
Finally, it steams over the horizon . . .
(I give it a push, and it falls to bits.
My doll sits in the mud at the bottom . . .)

From Sophie's Best Poetry book.

Killary seagull

Rosroe

The first person we saw in the quaint little hamlet, was Festy. He is the 'Old Rogue' of the village, known by all, and who can tell you all about the history of the hamlet. I showed him my two guardian dolls, Finbar and Finnuala, who are coming to stay at the cottage. He was very impressed.

The cottage was the same as always, shabby, comfortable, small and peaceful. There are three bedrooms, one for mummy and daddy, one for the children and one for Grannie and Granfer. Usually I sleep with my brothers in the children's room, but after Granfer had died there was a spare bed in Grannie's room. I am sleeping in the same room as Grannie, which is a real treat. On the mantelpieces there are shells and things that over the years children have collected. I have added some of mine – a big 'seashore' shell, and some oyster shells, all mother of pearl, and some little colourful ones. These are on Grannie's mantelpiece.

In the afternoon, Jeremy, mum and dad had a rest, so Oliver and me went over to Michael's Bay and collected lots of driftwood. We met some people from the youth hostel in Rosroe, and they were playing a guitar, a recorder, and singing hymns!

When we got back we went shrimping in the bay. When the tide went out far enough, we went shrimping in the rock pool. It was very good fun. Grannie's friend had left us a yummy fruit cake to eat. It is brilliantly tasty – I had a slice. I cannot believe that this time yesterday we were driving to Holyhead to catch the midnight ferry and then drove through the night until ten o'clock in the morning!

We are getting the boats out tomorrow. Oh, yes, mummy and I found a huge piece of fleece, and we are going to make some wool from it. Finbar and Finnuala are settling in nicely.

Sophie spent many family holidays in Connemara, staying in the family holiday cottage owned by her grandparents, Grannie and Granfer, in a beautiful coastal position near Killary Harbour, County Galway. Finbar and Finnuala are two rag dolls specially made with Grannie's help to live permanently in the cottage and look after it.

The dawn

I woke up at four o'clock and could not sleep at all. I think I dozed, for I remember nothing until . . . a twitter came to my ears, and another, and then one thousand voices of birds that seemed to say,

> "Look hence! Look hence!
> The dawn! The dawn!"

I looked out of the window and what a sight met my eyes!
The mountains in the distance, then the peninsular and then the lake, the sky flooded with light, and the sun came out, and that was the dawn.

Cooneenawaun Bay

As the very first streaks of light came over the horizon, he went down to the beach by the bay. As he got his boat the bay looked like a sea of glass. When he rowed out, the very first ripples were made. The sun peaked over the hills as he moored his boat and walked up the peninsular. A handsome sight was he sitting on a rock at the very end by the light of the sun, staring out to sea.

Sophie's Granfer would often set off early in the morning in his boat to go fishing.

I remember . . .

The wind swept the long grass to the East,
It whispered in the leaves of the trees,
And rushed over the water in the stream.
It crept through the window where clean glass once shone, and through the roof,
Where slates had long since fallen and sunk into the once well kept soil.
'Oh, to be young again!' the rotting boards sighed.
'Oh, to flow free again!' the choked stream cried.
Only phantom footsteps fall along the path to the house now.
An imaginary door opens,
As no-one walks into the once welcoming hall,
And silently the no-clock ticks against the faded wall.
'I remember . . .' sigh memories, long since gone.

A beautifully located abandoned cottage nearby may have inspired this poem.

About myself

I have nothing very interesting to write, but, because I have nothing very interesting to write about, I shall write about myself.

It is hard to describe oneself truthfully, I find, because some truths we do not like to admit. I am not the stereotype teenager. I do not make or maintain many friends easily, being too deep. I like my own company and have a fascination for the 'old way', (the romantic side) i.e.: candles, dip pens, sealing wax, shells, home cooking, herbal cures, dried flowers and secret passages.

I am one track minded – I get an idea set in my head and cannot change it. I am very disorganised and scatty. I cannot take practical jokes unless in a particularly good mood. I can be very bitchy without meaning to be. I can be very stubborn. I am musical, and can sing very well and act very well. I love reading, getting away from reality.

Aged fifteen.

Thoughts on love

I have come to a conclusion, Arion, about 'getting off'. Getting off can show no affection at all. When I got off with this boy, I didn't fancy him and I could tell that he didn't really care a toss for my character or what I was like inside. He was just bothered with my appearance which for some unknown reason he found attractive. The other boy, I think, was better – he did fancy me, but perhaps only because he was drunk, and I fancied him. I think he felt different in the morning!

No, I believe that in really caring relationships, just kissing is very nice. If my man were to gently, so gently, kiss me on the lips, and then on my cheeks, perhaps while music was playing, and then I kissed him back, so gently, until we kissed properly afterwards, and not straight 'into it', it would be so caring and so tender. I would just yearn for him, love him. That is how men who really care kiss their women and how women like to be loved.

My flat

My flat would be lovely. It would have planks on the floor. I would have borrowed some old rugs from home and bought some cheapo ones for it. There would be a chest of drawers for my clothes and a bed I had picked up in a junk shop. All the chairs would be painted a tasteful green colour and would be all different shapes and sizes, being cheap bargains from auctions, etc. I would have bought some brown, fiver a throw, cushions and covered them with nice material.

The walls would be white and I would have hung pictures of varying impressiveness on them. I would have one or two book cases stuffed with books and plays and things. There would be candles in candlesticks dotted about.

The cutlery in the kitchen would all be that cheap tin ware, except the mugs, of which there would be loads of different shapes.

There would be interesting oddments – like nice lamps and cruddy lamps and all my soft toys and my little writing desk. There would be a typewriter on the floor.

Out of the window I would have window boxes for my cooking herbs. I would have lots of green plants on the window ledges too. It would be great fun cooking interesting meals for one pound each, etc. Somewhere near my home would be a market and on Saturdays I could go and get my fresh vegetables and bargains – rugs and plates and things for my mobiles. I would have gone to Ireland and collected shells to string up in mobiles and as wall decorations.

I would have a bicycle with a big basket on the front. I might get the urge to go to Hyde Park for a picnic with a friend, or to the cinema or something.

I might wake up early and walk to a patisserie, and buy pain au chocolat and eat it when I got home with coffee.

I'd go to auditions when I wasn't working – perhaps as a secretary, perhaps as a waitress. It's debatable.

Sunglasses

In an attempt to escape reality
I put on the sunglasses,
Because my eyes were dazzled by life.
I grew used to their comforting dimness
And it was only when, many years later,
I remembered I was wearing them,
And found the courage to take them off,
That I realised what I had missed.

Aged fifteen.

We found several versions of this poem in her Log.

Old family photographs

I got into a real mess this evening because I looked at some old photos of Mummy and Daddy. They really affected me. I think it's the idea of time running away, and seeing children – carefree children – on paper before you, and the old adults next to them. I could hardly get over it. I burst into tears and Becca, dearest Becca, seemed to understand and I just sat there for ages crying.

It's the idea of so many days gone that were wasted or that I don't remember – each second moving and never there again; and that some day Mum and Dad will die, and some day I'll die; it's years and years away, but quick as a flash those years'll be gone and all that will be left of them is a pile of photos.

Aged sixteen.

Annie's Bar

Port Losta, Turkey.

I really don't want to forget this place because it would be an excellent basis and inspiration for a really nice and feasible life style. Annie is a Turkish lady who is about the nicest type of lady you can get. She's seen a bit of life and has obviously had her problems and has come up with a brilliant philosophy about how to live.

I think the best way to describe it is to describe the bar itself. It is a little white-washed building, two rooms deep, two rooms high, with a verandah in the front. The verandah is shaded by vines and various trees that wind in and out of the wicker frame covering the roof. Dotted around, hanging in the branches, are home-made oddments, mobiles made out of shells, tinfoil this-es and tinsel that-s.

There are candles in jam jars and dried grasses tucked into tin cans that have been brightened up with dabs of brightly coloured paint. The tables have cloths on them that Annie made herself – old pieces of sheeting, no money at all, tie-dyed (she has a small tie-dye business whereby she will sell tie-dyed garments or tie-dye your own for you for a price) and there you have it. Everywhere along the edge of the verandah are interesting stones and shells she has collected over the years.

The tables and chairs are wooden – not one matches. She has painted them all green so it doesn't matter. The tables are beautifully home-made – a bit bumpy and rickety. Again, none match. The whole place lets off an aura of comfort, slight disorder, and complete well-being and there is not one thing worth more than a few pennies – but it just doesn't matter, the whole place is just gorgeous.

Another thing about Annie's Bar are the animals. Turkish animals are generally thin, tick-ridden and miserable, but Annie's are all mellow and happy and there are loads of them. There are about four adult cats and several kittens, two or three dogs and last year there were a couple of tortoises.

She is not at all rich, but she is completely happy. Everyone loves her and she gets on with everyone. Her home is not fussy, but it is absolutely charming. I think she has an excellent attitude to life.

Stages in romance

1) G terms   (Greetings)
2) C terms   (Conversation)
3) H terms   (Hug)
4) KG terms   (Kiss G'bye)
5) DAO terms   (Drape All Over)
6) TC terms   (Total Comfort)

Aged sixteen.

Right, body, this is it

I have had enough of being fed up with my figure. I have the possibilities of a good figure here, but I abuse it by not doing enough exercise and by eating too much. I'm going to find out how much I weigh. By the end of term I'm going to weigh less. Let's be reasonable here. I have exams. So I can't be expected to diet seriously. But I can be expected to cut down in easy ways.

Eating –
> Breakfast:
> bran flakes/cereal, tea and fruit juice.
> Lunch:
> Salad, protein, one piece of bread, fruit.
> Supper:
> Healthy option, no chips, no in-betweens.

Exercise – some exercise every day.
> Minimum: ten sit ups and ten leg exercises on either side.
> Swimming: before breakfast.
> Sport: during day.
> Tennis, then jogging: after supper.

A week later – did I stick to it?

Did I heck!

Aged sixteen.

A Level choices

Dear Mum and Dad,

I promised I'd write this letter. I don't know if I'll ever finish it but I've taken the liberty of using a study period to start it at least.

Firstly, I'll remind you of what it is about. It is (I think) about why I want to carry on with drama as a career and why Theatre Studies A Level is important.

The thing about drama, and singing as well, is that it is something I love doing. I cannot not do it, if you see what I mean. I feel very daunted at the prospect of unemployment and let downs and so on, but it's just something I'll have to put up with, because I have to if it's a part of the job.

What I am afraid of is ending up just giving up the thought of acting, putting it to one side as a hobby and taking up a job I don't necessarily enjoy. It's a difficult thing, but I think there are really only two ways one can live one's life, either doing something you love despite the financial drawbacks, or doing something you don't mind and which gives you a reasonable and secure income. It's very dangerous of me to have said that because I don't have any experience of the 'real world'. It may be that as soon as I get out there, I'll realize what I fool I am and I'll settle down to English teaching or something. But I'm so unwilling to give up my dream, this dream that people are beginning to tell me may not be a complete impossibility. What Nick Hutchinson and my speech and drama teacher were saying about me is quite amazing. Nick said that I should carry on with acting as a career because he thinks I'd make a success of it. So does Mrs. Smith. I mean, it's really incredible. But they are saying it, and it makes me wonder if perhaps it's worth giving it a try.

I feel rather as if I'm being tested, and all these barriers are being put in my way to try and dissuade me. It's a good thing, because acting and singing are bitchy professions; they're hell. But if I can get through this time then I'll really be 'there'. It may be that I can't and people will persuade me that I should take more sensible A level subjects which will get me into a good university and a safe job. In which case, way hay, that's great. Because if I can get persuaded, that's the best thing that could possibly happen, so that I don't jump out and make a fool of myself because I'm not one hundred per cent for acting and singing. But if I do get through it then it'll prove that I am in there one hundred per cent, and that is also great.

Being at St. Swithun's these past years has been a major lump of the test. So many of my friends said how they wanted to be actresses in the lower fourth, who, when they didn't get the main part in 'Daisy' or 'Annie' gave up and now think they may be a lawyer. I got so frustrated because I couldn't be in those plays.

But, unlike ninety five per cent of the school, it didn't stop me. "But I really to do want to be an actress", I might say and a teacher would pat me on the head and say, "yes, dear." But that has just made me all the more keen. There is a definite difference. And Mrs. Sherlock said to me last September she could see how frustrated I was. She had practically been watching for me to come because eventually everyone truly keen did – people like Sam Line!

The point is people have tried to squash me over and over again but I won't be. I'll prove that to you.

Sophie was sixteen when she wrote this.

Hurrah for Edward

I phoned Edward today, and we talked for ages. I'm so happy. He and I have spent a year disagreeing and arguing, and now we really get on quite wonderfully. He asked my advice on things, and was interested in my response. He told me his plans, and shared with me a piece of advice to take criticism/insults and praise exactly the same way, and keep your eye on the ball. We've really got it sorted. I know we can tease each other and criticise each other and admit faults to each other, and have a laugh. I can't believe it, after all that happened last year. Wowee! I slept till late and did very little all day, and I love this pen, it writes so smoothly! Hurrah for me & hurrah for Edward darling!

Edward and Sophie were good friends and this letter refers to their discussions about directing plays. This was written when Sophie was sixteen.

Sophie had a leading part in a production of Damn Yankees at Winchester College. Photograph by Clive Barda.

A really nice boy

I met a really nice boy today. I mean really nice. He is funny and genuine and open. He isn't "hey! I'm so cool", or shy. He's pleasant looking and has beautiful puppy dog eyes. He was really nice to me and I had a heart to heart with him about Dward while playing boxes. Then we went outside to look at the stars and touched on subjects I find really interesting - infinity, stuff like that. He plays the guitar and I sang along to his playing some songs and it felt so right - I mean, we seemed to hit it off really well. The thing is that I have to be careful, because I have only known him 24 hours - long enough to know I think he's one of the nicest people I've met. Also long enough to know he's not out for the catch. He is too genuine and faithful to snog anyone while he fancies this one girl from home. Also I have to remember this. Girl friend/boyfriend relationships to do not last. They always go wrong. However if nothing sexual happens a boy and girl may very easily be really close friends. It's also a lot maturer to be able to like someone and be good friends with them without assuming that sexual relations are expected, or necessary. I mean, if you, as soon as you start liking a boy, snog him, you know each other too well physically, but not well enough mentally, and the gossip aroused by your getting off puts pressure on you and puts a strain on your relationship, and more often than not it falls through. So, course of action with this boy:

– meet him socially a few times.
– to do a play with him?
– FORGET ROMANCE
– DON'T TELL ANYONE YOU LIKE HIM
– see how things naturally progress.

The thing was that last night we even touched on the subject of it being hard for boys and girls to have a relaxed relationship: much better to be good friends. The other thing is that he is nice to everyone, not just me. He treated me the same as everyone else, perhaps with a teeny bit more reserve because he doesn't know me as well as most of the others there. So it goes to show that he doesn't 'fancy' me. I am glad. Because I really like him and if anything progresses from here, even friendship, which is ten times better than lust, it must be founded on friendship and mutual interests. Like music. And acting. And a sense of humour. And deeptalk. Anyway, he must see me in my nicest light. I musn't be selfish or show off in his presence. So I won't. I will not be weak. Show high principles. They never go wrong. Oh, I would value his special friendship so much right now. So I must keep it to myself. (Yuh, right.)

Aged sixteen

This was an increasingly happy time for Sophie. She was well-established and respected in school and outside as a talented actress and singer. She was awarded a place in the National Youth Choir of Great Britain. She had made deep and valued friendships.
Her life was full with singing, acting and directing commitments, with her 'A' levels, English Literature, Theatre Studies, Religious Studies and much else besides.

After she left school in July 1997, she was thrilled to be cast in the National Youth Theatre's production of Romeo and Juliet in the small but important part of the Duke Escalus, which she played as a woman. The 'Time Out' reviewer commended her for her dignified performance.

On the strength of unexpectedly good A Level results she set her sights on a place at Magdalen College, Oxford, to read English. She spent the following few months preparing herself for the Oxford interview, working as a waitress in the village pub and giving drama workshops to youngsters in a nearby school.

Just before her death she was planning her strategy to direct and produce a friend's play at the next Edinburgh Festival Fringe, hoping to involve several of her National Youth Theatre friends in the project.

Chapter Three

Maturing

Sophie reflects

We sat in my room and talked.
Thousands of words
Passed between us.
I became confused
Who was talking.
It was as if
I'd looked in the mirror
and found someone looking through the other side,
Someone with dark hair.

Aged seventeen.

Venice

It is places like Venice that prove a source of inspiration to people. There is nowhere like it in the world.

I would like, one day, to spend two weeks wallowing in Venice, on my own. That way I could spend timeless hours savouring each church, each back alley. I could sit in some shady cafe by the Grand Canal and write letters to people, or read, or write poetry. I could go to bed early or stay up all night, wandering along the streets and canal ways of Venice. I could sit in some shady corner and watch the tourists flow past me, day after day.

I would like to leisurely discover the history of Venice, not just the physical history, but the history of the Art and the places where poets stood. I want to stand on the Bridge of Sighs just before dawn and discover for myself the essence of the name. I should like to be at leisure not to have to think, but just to exist, at peace with myself and the rest of the world.

Aged seventeen.

Sophie went on a tour of Florence and Venice with the St. Swithun's School Senior Choir.

Grandfather's things

It is wonderfully peaceful up here. One forgets how peaceful it is. This house is full of beautiful family things, and Dad says that Grandmother thinks Grandfather's spirit is in this house. I think she might be right and it is certainly an understandable belief. I think that when a loved one dies it must be the hardest thing in the world to accept. Also, what does one to do with all their things? There is a picture in a leather case of Grandmother as a young woman, that Grandfather must have had in his wallet during the war. What did Grandmother do with it when she discovered it? She put it in Grandfather's desk. Special things – diaries and photos and trinkets and books – that meant nothing to Grandmother – she may not even have known of their existence – and everything to Grandfather. Now he has died, what is she to do with them? Throwing them away is impossible, keeping them, useless. And yet . . .

Aged eighteen.

Kindertransport

Kinderstransport. First performance. How do I feel? Like any amateur director after the first performance of their first play, with the knowledge that it is only a third over. A bit flat. There is a sob in my throat that won't go away.

It went really well. The actresses were terrific. I enjoyed it immensely and the lighting finally worked well, the sound worked well. There was an audience of about forty. Now everyone needs to stay motivated.

My life has revolved around KT. It is going to be weird at the end of the week having nothing left to do. I have tried to prepare myself but the hollow feeling is already starting. I feel very pleased though, because we really proved what can be done with our school hall facilities. Ed came to see the dress rehearsal yesterday. He was very complimentary about it. And it was so bad yesterday! Hurrah is all I can say.

Sophie directed Kindertransport by Diane Samuels, as part of her A Level Theatre Studies course, when she was eighteen.

Amy, m'dear

Amy, m'dear –

It sounds like you are having a ball in Australia. I'm absolutely green with envy. How long have you been in Australia then? It sounds like the ultimately dreamy place to be. What do you think? Maybe I should go there for my GAP. I don't know, I haven't decided. There's so much stuff I want to do. Last holidays I went to New York with my parents. It was absolutely amazing, dreamy, superb. I felt like I was walking into a film! Everyone had the accent. It was so weird. I only saw a minuscule bit of America but I think I'd like to go back and travel there. A student friend of mine went there a while back and said it was fab, but that you couldn't have the best time until you were twenty one because of the drinking laws and stuff. So maybe I'll head out to Aussieland for my GAP and travel America 'Thelma and Louise style' after university . . .

I've been racking my small brain and searching my heart about what to do with my life! I think you may have to be upset because I think I want to be a famous director, not an actor . . . er . . . you see the thing is I took the Junior Drama Club last term and discovered that one of the most stimulating things I've ever done was to do with directing kids . . . so the latest plot is to get a drama degree –hopefully —and head off to a town and start up a county Youth Theatre, like Oxfordshire Youth Theatre. It's so exciting, Amy, because I know that I can and it's so possible and other people want to do it too so aaaaaah! The great thing about drama is there is so much scope and so much variety. You can do anything.

FATHER's DAY IN NEW YORK

Written when Sophie was seventeen.

All's well

Darling Mum and Dad,

I am at this moment in time sitting on my bed in my box (study/bedroom). It's dark outside so I've drawn the curtain. In the background I can hear Eric Clapton playing quietly and mellowly on my tape recorder and my room has the faintly untidy look that accompanies me – and every Saturday afternoon – after I've been to town. And you know what? I am utterly happy. I'm happy with myself, my life, you, my darling parents, my brothers, my work situation (almost), my box, my friends, my teachers, er, and lots of other things.

I really feel that at last, last, last I've found my niche and established myself properly. Of course I have my little grumbles – don't we all – but I rather enjoy them, strangely. I mean, I am doing pretty well here. I've got lots of friends and I'm a music scholar and an academic scholar.

Dear Grannie

Thank you so much for your letter. I'm really glad that you enjoyed the concert so much. I certainly enjoyed singing it. Doing the solo in the New Hall has always been an ambition of mine, and all I can think is how incredibly lucky I am to be given the opportunity to fulfil so many of my ambitions: National Youth Theatre, 'Equus', The Southampton Festival under 19's Drama Championship (I won!), an academic scholarship, a trip to New York ... what an amazingly lucky person I am.

Sometimes I worry that my share of luck is surely due to run out. And then something else good happens. Goodness knows I deserve a bit of disappointment and so on. Still, as an actress I'm sure I have plenty of disappointments to look forward to before I really succeed.

Thank you for all your encouraging words. I'm very lucky (again!) for having a Gran like you. You're really very special.

Anyway, I must get on with some work. I'm sorry I don't write as regularly as I should. I'm so busy at the moment! I look forward to seeing you very soon.

All my love, from your
                    Sophie X

Aged seventeen.

Lower Fourth Form Drama Club

I am going to be allowed to take the Junior Drama Club after half term. There are various aspects of theatre I want to get across to these girls.

Ensemble theatre is as important as single roles. You cannot have a good production if every actor is fighting for the attention of the audience, instead of supporting each other. In my workshops, there will be no lead parts, just a group development.

I remember going to Drama Club and being told to pretend to be a flower, or to mime climbing up mountains. But all along I wanted to do what I called 'real acting' – getting stuck into proper plays and doing 'serious' drama. I thought I was being patronised by being expected to do such infantile things.

However, I have since learned that creative, non-naturalistic, symbolic acting and drama is extremely exciting, and a very impressive skill.

So I am going to use my knowledge from the National Youth Theatre to show these girls how actors use mime, and that to mime, etc. is a very useful skill. I think that my being a member of the VIth form will make me more accessible, and my N.Y.T.-ship will make them listen to what I have to say.

I would like to encourage people's assertiveness, to give everyone a chance to act in front of their friends, and to ask questions as much as they like. Hopefully this will help them develop into less sheep-like members of the school and show them individuality is something to be proud of.

I would like to use pieces of image-filled poetry and plays, and work around them to create a piece of drama and movement.

Aged seventeen.

Sophie ran drama workshops for younger girls at school and later as a Gap Year job in a local school.

Thoughts on drama

I have enjoyed drama since I was eight years old. For ten years, I have wanted to be an actress, stubbornly assuring my teachers as much. In 1995 I got a place in the National Youth Theatre and the introductory course changed my outlook totally. We did a lot of physical drama, and experimented with portraying emotions through physical analogy. Our project was based on the loss of a loved one.

Drama, for me, is a way of showing people home truths, and experimenting with ideas that I feel strongly about. I took the Junior Drama Club at school, and found directing children, whose minds are so imaginative and uninhibited, immensely fulfilling and exciting. I found it easy to adapt my artistic ideas to their age, and as I have always loved working with kids, I was very successful. With drama, I have enormous drive. I find it easy to focus myself and try out new ideas.

On N.Y.T. I learnt a lot about group cooperation, and as a result I realized that much more stimulating than taking the limelight was being part of a team. I find the group spirit, that I have only experienced in drama, almost psychological. We were all tuned directly into each other. I should like to recreate that with other people, especially children, because I believe that to be the key of good drama. That, and a vivid imagination and the courage to speak out.

My work experience at Chichester Festival Theatre showed me theatre at its most commercial. I enjoyed it enormously, but talking to the actors and directors made me realize that I wanted to do more than produce that which the audience will pay for because they know and understand it.

Drama is an essential part of me. I am lost without it, and I want to pioneer my ideas, even if I have no money and have to live in a tent. I would be being untrue to myself if I denied myself the chance to create drama.

Aged seventeen.

Hecate

On being alone at a railway station

A strange grey town
Blotted out by night;
Deep voids of crowded air,
A flickering neon sign,
A deserted platform.
Across the other side,
On red benches no-one sits.
The box clock ticks, echoes
In the brimming space.
Flick, a minute passes.

But more –
People hurry to rain flecked cars
Enclosed in metal,
Relieved and going home.
An image of evening –
Television, warmth, food.
People beyond yellow squares,
Who see no rivulet stranger.
A barrier of space makes her
Untouchable.
(Sitting in the dust, fierce sun,
Fire wounds sweet smelling death)

And more –
People drain away to duvets
The streets, full of no-one,
Transform.
As her tired footsteps pass,
Blank building faces
Are dispassionate judges.
Under their gaze, people
Draw in, shiver, scurry
To bolt holes, protection.
Hurry in the hostile air.
Night streets are no place for people.

And more.
Yellow black clouds
Blanket thick, sinking
Sludge on the station.
And trains, vast heaves
Of agonising noise –
A flicker of faces, coffee cups,
Framed by black –
Flick flick flick swoosh
Gone. Wind in her fingers.
The dark resignation hunches.
There are no trains stop here tonight.

Sophie Large

Aged eighteen.

Sophie frequently travelled on trains between home and school and on her many other excursions.

From Sophie's Best Poetry book.

A good party needs:

Nice hosts – to make you feel welcome and comfortable.

Old faces for reassurance and new faces for interest and potential.

A marquee, because of the smart party atmosphere.

A good band and dance floor so everyone can dance as much as they want to.

Munchies, so no one is ever hungry, even at midnight.

A smart dinner is just really, really nice.

Lots of booze at appropriate times, i.e. champagne beforehand, white/red/pudding wines with dinner, etc.

No curfew – so everyone can stay the night in relative comfort and enjoy a complete party experience, not just an incomplete, mildly unsatisfying short one.

Speeches. Um. Why? Speeches add atmosphere and common talking ground.

Dressing up makes one feel more attractive and thus confident.

A warm place to go – without which one would feel unwelcome/uncomfy/cold.

A party needs to be organised down to the last detail. Voila!

Sophie's 18th birthday party invitation

You are invited to

'The End of Summer Party'

To celebrate Sophie Large's 18th Birthday
At Home: 17, Silver St., Chacombe, Banbury Oxon From:
The Evening of September 1st until the Morning of September 2nd.
An outside Dinner, Pimm's, Music,
Champagne, Strawberries on the Lawn...
Please bring a bottle of something sparkly, a tent and a toothbrush-
a Tennis racket an option...
RSVP before July 15th also for information and Guest list.

Dress: Smart--Summery

Ode to John Coltrane

A rich warm August night,
round tables on the lawn,
low witty discerning chatter,
strong French cigarette smoke,
candle light, the stars,
evening dress, champagne.
Fairy lights in the trees reflected on the river,
no breeze, not a flicker of a candle flame.
Laughter
And behind it all, in low, artistic rhythm,
are heard the strains of
John Coltrane.

This is now

We were all outside
And I, lingering, came last.
The night air caressed me
And held me in its balmy embrace.
I heard you all laughing ahead,
And, unafraid, I felt alone.
And I looked at the lights
Sparkling on the sea. And I
looked long at the clear moon,
Almost full, silver and remote.
And suddenly I felt a huge
sense of the present.
The feelings flooded though me:
I felt that I had so nearly
Touched the untouchable.
I shrugged away the feeling of loss,
And contentment, like wine,
Smooth and clear and sweet,
Filled my soul,
And I said, as I followed you,
A long way behind:
"This is now."

Parents

Darling mum and dad,

Hello there. How are you both? I expect by the time you receive this I will have spoken to you on the phone; but I wanted to write. Probably the first letter I've sent you from school in a long time!

I want to thank you for giving me that money. It is really extremely generous of you, and I want you to know that I will not spend it on anything I think I ought to pay for myself. I am sorry and extremely annoyed at myself for asking you for a raise in my allowance in the first place, because you give me an ample amount as it is, and if I run out, well, it should be my look out, shouldn't it?! It's part of being a student, never having loads of money!

It can be so easy to take things for granted, and overlook things that are important. When one is in a bad mood, you can forget to be grateful. Sometimes I forget that you are sending me to this wonderful school and take J & O and me (whoops) on glorious holidays, and buy us expensive new ski suits, as well as giving us all generous allowances. Please forgive me for being so selfish and ungrateful for all you both to do to make my life as wonderful as it is.

I want you to know that even if you both didn't, or couldn't, give me a bean, I would love you both just as much as I do now. Money is such a small part of it. It's the little things that mean so much more – understanding my moods, poking my tummy in the middle of the night, flowers by my bed. You are both the most wonderful parents anyone could hope for. I mean that, dad, I'm not being "thespy"!

I think that being a parent must be one of the most testing, painful, heart rending, and yet rewarding (I hope!) jobs in the world. I hope very much that one day I'll be able to be a parent something as good as you two.

Everything's going spiffingly here. I've got a lie-in tomorrow, which is a blessing! This weekend I've loads to do, including preparation for my pilot Monday evening drama workshop, and an awful lot of nasty essays to be done for Monday ... I received four letters on the day I got back to school, which was really cheering. One from my Aussie man, Tim! Hurrah! Australia backpacking holiday, here I come, wooooo!

Anyway, I must go to bed. So keep smiling, and I'll see you soon – from your loving daughter Sophie

Written when Sophie was seventeen.

Career planning

I looked up careers choices all day today. I think what I would like to do at the moment is get an English & Drama degree, at Hull, Bristol, or U.E.A, then go to Drama college and try acting as a career. That's six more years of education. And then if all that failed I'd train as a drama therapist. So:

1997	A levels	18
1998	Gap year	19
1999	University	20
2000	University	21
2001	University	22
2002	Working	23
2003	Drama college	24
2004	" "	25
2005	" "	26
2006	trying to succeed	27
2007	at acting	28
2008	Drama therapy course	29
2009	" "	30
2010	practising drama therapist	31

Omigod. But I don't see how I can get round it.

Um. That's about all.

Aged seventeen.

Dear Will

The second message in your book my darling, and possibly the last, but hey – maybe not. I don't feel I ever had the chance to really talk to you but I know you will always mean something to me, because few people really appreciate the stars. I am going to remember you every time there is a cold starry night somewhere in England. Do you have a song that you associate with stars, my darling? Do you think you are going to make sure you have a fab life? I remember you telling me your plans and I know you will always be successful and happy. I want to be successful, I want to make my life fun and happy, but – do you know what? I am trying to be profound and I just can't right now. I am going to miss lots of things about Winchester and Swithun's – Illumina and Q.E.II Shagwagg concerts, drinking furtive beers after Equus rehearsals. The music in Equus, do you remember it? That was fab, I'm going to miss you a whole load. I'm looking forward to getting away and getting on with stuff. When I'm famous, Will, I'll take you out to dinner in some discerning London bar and we'll talk deep again.

See you, my darling.

Aged eighteen.

Sophie wrote this entry in a friend's diary just before she left school.

Good Luck my darling
I know you can do it!

On being alone, outside, on a summer night

The warm treacle day dissolves,
Mellows to ruby red Port wine.

The night glides and smooths
In deep contented dreamings

I drift into the garden folds,
Lie still in cool moist grasses. Now

The finite world around me stirs,
I seep within its slow rhythm;

The air flows clear; is full
Of serene, boundless stillness. Yet

My eyes search high heights, through leafy
Boughs of darkened summer trees.

The whole sky soars down to me,
Droves of streaks of invisible.

My mortality aches in me,
Stretches sobbing to its core

Before this vast weeping space
My smallness smalls and crumples more

The skies are mourning for me
With countless white tears!

Running limbs flicker in the moonlight,
Grasses part and swish and crackle.

Something turns – some cavity
Deep within lets free its captive

Those thoughts reluctant from me
Break away, away in night breezes

Grieving black, of a sudden,
Return to air, retracts its lull.

My mind, deceptive slow, snaps back –
The red wine of my being thrills –

Behind me trail strange wonderings
In darkness lonely, unconfessed.

My whole being mirthful rings.
Not yet, I say. Don't mourn me yet!

Aged eighteen.

From Sophie's Best Poetry book.

Ode to waiting for a call

Oh my heart weeps
Oh my soul is stone
As I sit sobbing by the telephone
I plead and cry and beg
The plastic telephone
But it is no use
No matter how I moan;
For sadly, sadly,

(Perhaps the phone did ring . . .)

This was found scribbled in the back of a telephone directory. A friend identified the handwriting. It must have been written a year or two earlier.

Ode to waiting for a Call.

Oh my heart weeps
Oh my soul is stone
As I sit sobbing
By the Telephone
I plead and cry and beg
The plastic telephone
But it is no use
No matter how I moan;
For sadly, sadly,

Surprise A Level results

11 am.

I get my A level results back in one hour. Oh my God. What is going to be the outcome? Were any of my papers worth an A Grade? What if I get B's and C's? Then where will I be? And what will the B be in? Theatre Studies? If so, what a wasted opportunity. Or even English, considering the paper was so poor.

12.30 pm

Four A's!
I don't know what to think! I mean, first of all I think how incredibly lucky I am. There were papers I did that I should not have got A's for. The General Studies must have been so easy to pass!

Then I think, my God! The world is my oyster! I could go to Oxford, I can take a gap year and to do all those things I want to do – get a computer qualification, some work. Then disappear off around Australia or something, maybe America, and afterwards go to Oxford or at least Bristol. I mean, I can do anything now that I have got the grades! I feel like the hugest weight has been lifted off my shoulders.

Aged eighteen.

Youth theatre plans

My initial list of Practical Planning.

1) Write to people who may have advice or information on the subject.

2) Write to the Banbury Arts Council to see where we stand with them.

3) Write to Banbury Arts Centre to see how they feel about the idea and if they mind.

4) If they sound positive, walk around Banbury and ask public opinion about the idea, with a questionnaire.

5) Find guidance about the best way to make the plan legit and official. i.e. make it charity status, ask about insurance, necessary qualifications etc.

6) Write to English and Drama departments of schools and ask to come and take workshops with the students.

7) With teachers and students, organise a weekly slot when students can come for a drama session.

8) Make a publicity flyer, send them to schools, youth clubs etc.

9) Organise a two week slot in the Summer holidays when people can come on a course.

10) Write and phone local businesses and ask them for sponsorship. Local radio advertising.

11) Find a venue – the Arts space, or a Village Hall, or wherever.

12) Set up the course.

Boogy.

Written when Sophie was nineteen; she planned to start a Youth Theatre for local children.

Oh my God, Hannah!

Oh, my God, Hannah,

Last night was so cool. As you know I went up to London, and saw lots of cool actor people. Hahahaha. I was so nervous that the play would fall flop on their heads, especially as Edward said after he read it that he thought it was really rather poor. They were expecting genius, and thankfully, genius they got! They all giggled their heads off, cried a lot. They loved it! We were like excited children about to go to Disneyland! I've only ever read it to myself before; and yes I chortled and appreciated it, but it was only when hearing it read aloud with characterisation that all the lines came alive off the page, and you saw the real subtlety and genius of Jon's writing. I am so excited! I still am fully aware that it all needs major goings-over. But the great great great thing is that the actors loved it and will go and tell their friends how much they loved it. It is just terrific. And Hannah they were all really afraid to meet me! Hahahah! and Simon the fit one said to Emily after the audition that he really, really, really, had to be in it and had to be involved and had to be in it and had to be in it!
HAHAHAHAAHAHAHAHAHAAHHAAAAAAAAAAAAAAAAAAAA!!!!!
RAAAAAAAAAAAAAAOOOOOOOOOAAAAAAAAAAAAAAAAHHHHHHHHHHHHH
I AM INVINCIBLE! And then we sat around until late at night. I am knackered thru and thru– had to get up at 0500 for the 0630 train back this morning, in time for 3 hours secretarial college this morning.
AAAAAAAAAAAAAAAAWWWWW

An e-mail to a girlfriend. Sophie had just been seeing some National Youth Theatre friends in London. She was nineteen and planned to take Jon Groom's new play 'Pope-Afloat' to the next Edinburgh Festival Fringe.

Tender love

My darling

When all my life runs and rattles round me like a whirlwind, I shall think of you, like a memory yet to happen. I could love you my dearest. Your character, charming, funny, open, innocent, humorous; your looks, beautiful brown eyes smiling. The fact that we can run and fool around like two-year-olds. Maybe one day I shall love you. But now we must do our own thing – make our mistakes, our triumphs, our ambitions. You must have sordid teenage affairs and I must have sordid university lovers. But I think in the neutral sphere of the Oxfordshire countryside, where pressures are nil and where holidays reign – there, we shall always be bound together, unknowing (on your part) and we shall return to each other many years from now. I shall maybe love you as a mere, comforting, secure memory of times that have not happened yet. Long, late summer afternoons, drowsing with insects in the still air . . .

Oxford agony

I did not get into Oxford. No more chances, This is a failure I shall have to live with. I wish I were going to Edinburgh now, far away from the site of my shame. I feel so frustrated. In the interview I gave them a negative vibe. I failed to tell them about any of the exciting stuff I've been doing. I was rubbish. They saw a mediocre loser, when I was, am, so fabulous. I still can't believe some of the s*** I told them, and all the opportunities I had to shine and didn't. If I knew I had given it my best shot, and hadn't got in, I would not mind so much. But I didn't.
I gave it a pathetic, flustered, confused and half-hearted shot, and did not get in.
I will never know whether I would have got in if I had given it my best shot.
And that is the worst feeling. I am now consigned to the ranks of Oxford wannabe's. When people ask if I got into Oxford, my family will have to say "no, but she's going to Bristol" – and the people will say "ah" and think to themselves uhuh, Oxford wannabe, less than Oxford.

James said to me, Sophie – you're bigger than Oxford. I hope this is true. I'm also very bitter and angry. Perhaps this is fate. It's the half heartedness of the interview which infuriates me the most; the fact that those tutors must have thought, no, mediocre. Not interested. And there is no way I can ever make them see how wrong they are. What a moan.

Aged nineteen.

E-mail to Abi

Dear Abi,
hey there babes! How are you? Did you have a good vac? I have loads to talk to you about, are you around this Saturday for a cheapy lunch? Cos as you may know I am organising a play to Edinburgh this summer and want to see if you would like to get involved. Anyway I'd like to pick your considerable brains! Tragically I did not get into Oxford but don't worry I'm not bitter and I feel fine about it all. I have had a brilliant holiday, and want to hear all about yours. So – Hope you read your email occasionally, do get back in touch soooon.
loads of love, Sophie Large x x x

Silver Lining Theatre Company

Business Idea:
to create a viable, exciting theatre company
to produce a play at the Edinburgh Festival Fringe
to be recognised as an entrepreneur of modern theatre

Business Mission Statement:
Financially:
to break even and be able to keep the theatre running after this summer
Personally:
to bring together talented young people who I admire and to create an extraordinary theatre experience.

We found an application form completed by Sophie requesting a business bank account for the Silver Lining Theatre Company.

A day before her accident she had prepared offer letters to the actors she wanted to cast in the play.

Dear Simon

The Silver Lining Theatre Company

9th February, 1998

Dear Simon,

Thank you very much for auditioning for the forthcoming production of 'Pope-Afloat' by Jonathan Groom. On behalf of the Silver Lining Theatre Company I am very pleased to offer you the part of Derek.

You will be called for rehearsals from July 11th to July 31st, and will be required in Edinburgh from August 3rd to August 24th. The play is expected to run from August 9th to 23rd. As well as acting in the play you will be expected to aid publicity campaigns in Edinburgh before and during the two weeks. Any other dates involving preliminary rehearsals and meetings before July will be mailed to you and the rest of the cast in letters updating you on the progress of the Company.

Despite the fact that we intend to run Silver Lining as professionally as possible, this is nevertheless an amateur production. We will therefore be unable to pay you for your part in the play beyond an equal share in the proceeds after all other expenses have been paid. Regrettably there is no way we can guarantee that our fund-raising will cover all your costs. Therefore what we are unable to subsidise you will have to pay yourself. We are optimistic that accommodation and travel will be partially if not completely subsidised as they are priorities in the budget. There will be fund-raising events held during the vacations. Any help you can give towards these would be greatly appreciated. The more money raised the less it will cost each person to perform in Edinburgh. As a safety measure we are also asking all people involved in the production to send us a deposit of £50 to be returned on 24th August 1998. Let me emphasise that these deposits will not go towards the production funds and will be returned if and when your commitment to the Company for the 1998 season is fulfilled.

The priority for the next couple of months is mainly bureaucratic. You will be kept informed about the progress of Silver Lining during this time. Once the script has been completed you will of course be sent a copy. This is likely to be within the next few weeks. It is only later on this year that the actual creativity can commence so until then I thank you for your patience! **Please** could you return the enclosed form to me as soon as possible. Once it is returned I will be able to formalise with the Central School your place with the Company. If you have any questions please do not hesitate to call me.

I think this project is going to be hugely exciting with such a talented and impressive group of people involved and I very much hope to be able to work with you in the summer. Thanks again and best wishes,

Yours sincerely

Sophie Large

Sophie Large
Artistic Director

We found this poem on a sheet of paper on Sophie's desk in her beautiful bedroom on the day that she died. She had made one or two corrections the weekend before to a draft written when she was about seventeen. How lovely to know she was having these deep thoughts just before she died.

A sniff of the real me

Somewhere floating above reality,
In time and space and place,
I exist. The real me
Stretches, and yawns, waking
Like a cat from oblivion,
Or an animal from hibernation.

The real me swirls and wavers,
Like a half remembered memory
Or a tune, once heard, now forgotten.
I move silently across my mind;
Behind my eyes, under my nose:
My ears hear me acutely.

I, me, myself, am real, alive, here.
I enjoy the feel of life under my hand,
The shouting and screaming,
The mad abandoned laughter of one
Who has let go of the parts of her mind
That hold the real her prisoner.

Feelings I want to feel
But would never dare to admit
Fill me up and drink me in like wine:
Sensual, sweet, intoxicating,
And I wallow in their rays,
Basking in the delight of release.

People ask her personal questions,
And smilingly she lies. But the real me
Cannot lie: I feel things, experience things
Too potent and wonderful to be wrong,
And my mind screams out the truth
While
    My mouth smiles,
    My head shakes,
    My lips are still.

Written in Sophie's Best Poetry book.

Sophie Large, biographical notes

1978 – 1998

Schools

The Carrdus School, Overthorpe Hall, Banbury; Winchester House School, Brackley; St. Swithun's School, Winchester.

Drama/acting

God in *Noyes Fludde*; Koong Se in *The Willow Pattern*; Sarah Brown in *Guys and Dolls*; finalist in *Shakespeare on the Platform*; Barbara Jackson in *Pack of Lies*; Hesther Salomon in *Equus*; Meg Boyd in *Damn Yankees*; Escalus in *Romeo and Juliet,* a National Youth Theatre production.

Drama/directing

War on the Home Front written by Kate Bolwell, co-directed with Sarah Copas; *Kindertransport* by Diane Samuels; Artistic Director designate of *Pope-Afloat* by Jon Groom, a Silver Lining Theatre Company production.

Singer

Chorus: *The Pearl Fishers*; Soprano, St. Swithun's Senior Choir; Soprano soloist: *The Chichester Psalms*; Soprano, The National Youth Choir of Great Britain.

Poet

Senior Silver Medalist Award for Spoken Poetry, The Poetry Society; author of *Innocence, Imagination, A Sniff of the Real Me, Catkins, Sunglasses, The Pleasant Scents of Spring, Catastrophically Speaking, On Being Alone Outside on a Summer Night,* and many other poems.

Writer

Author of many stories, diaries, letters, etc.

Teacher

Drama workshop teacher at The Carrdus School during gap year.

Sadie Large

INDEX

REVIEWS

Susan Hill, The Mail on Sunday

All children are special. So it is not surprising that when Sophie Large's family found a cache of poems and prose after she was killed in a car accident, aged 19, they thought them clear signs of a fledgling literary talent. All parents who lose a child want somehow to see that child immortalised and have something good come out of their destruction. Sophie's Log is published in aid of a fund established in her name for aspiring singers and actors. Sophie acted, played, sang . . . and wrote. She was a thoughtful dreamer and, as dreamers do, often felt isolated, different. Writing helped. The everyday hopes and disappointments Sophie describes speak directly to our own adult memories of what it is like to be a teenager. They are lively, touching, sometimes revelatory, but also typical of the sort of things so many girls like her write. And that is the whole point: that's why the young will respond to them and the rest of us can learn something from them.

Sophie's writings, such as the poem "Sunglasses", are a way into her mind and heart. The Sophies are oysters we have no right to prise open, yet we need to discover what makes them tick to understand them. Just in case they need us suddenly. It is always hard being young, and more so now. The pressures are greater.

Sophie was talented and got excellent A-levels but Oxford rejected her. The hurt and defensiveness are keenly expressed. Her writings reveal not just a vibrant young women, but a true representative of young people. She holds up a torch for them, but by its light the rest of us can see a little better too. This book brings Sophie to life for us – the lovely, laughing girl on the cover. She looks quite like my own daughter, a year her senior. Like so many other rare and special spirits.

That's why her book is important.

Joanna Trollope

This is an extraordinary and moving anthology. It is extraordinary because it is so transparently honest. The writing in it is by a girl who had remarkable self knowledge and a quiet self-confidence from a very young age. It is moving not simply because of the inexpressibly sad fact that Sophie is dead, but even more because it reveals those joys and despairs and hopes and longings that most people lack the courage to reveal – reading these pages makes one feel the honoured recipient of Sophie's trust. She was plainly someone of considerable and varied emotional depth, great imagination, great sweetness and charm and – this comes out above all and illuminates the book – a huge relish for life. As a consequence, her log is full of an energy that will be, in the end I think, her most vivid testimonial. The whole book is proof – if proof were ever needed for such a thing – that nothing lovely is ever wasted. It will give heart to the young who, like her, have set their hearts on a special and difficult path in life; and comfort to all those who need to know that, even after a desperate grief, life can be worth living again.

Lindsay Frazier, Guardian Education Supplement

Sophie Large was killed, aged 19, in a car crash. In her memory, her parents have published many of her letters, poems, diary entries and even emails in order to raise funds for Sophie's Silver Lining Fund, which supports young would-be actors and singers. Sophie's Log (£7 inc p&p from TheLarges@aol.com) presents a picture of a caring, committed, delightful and very human being. Teenagers will find their own worlds reflected in her thoughts, her enthusiasms and her sadder moments.

Juliet Townsend, childrens' book reviewer, The Spectator

Sophie Large comes alive in her own pages as a strong and unusual personality; imaginative, observant, energetic and thoughtful. She is an excellent and lively letter writer with an unusual gift for writing interestingly, about ideas as well as events. Some of her early poems are curiously old fashioned. They read like the work of a young girl who has read and been influenced by a lot of old children's books. Perhaps her awareness of the past and her sympathy with older people explain why she was sometimes out of step with what seemed at the time the all important "loads of trendies" at her school. Sophie overcame these difficulties, largely through her achievements in music and drama. Her zest and energy are infectious and do something to explain the impact her loss had on all those who knew her. No life can be more than absolutely full – Sophie's short life was as full or fuller than many which have lasted four times as long. In this collection we can see her developing from the derivative writing of early childhood to find her own voice – a voice which sings.

Gillian Clarke, Times Educational Supplement

Sophie's Log is an unusual book. Sophie Large was killed in a road accident when she was 19. Here are 27 poems, with notebook extracts, letters, journal entries and e-mails to friends, arranged chronologically. Most collected works gathered in memoriam by a family for a dead child or spouse make poor reading, but this book is as appealing as a diary. Although this is not a classic – such as the Diary of Anne Frank – it appeals for its ordinariness, for expressing the inner life of a typical, though brighter-than-average, girl, from the word-loving child to the ambitious would-be theatre director who fails to get into Oxford. Sophie's ambition, breathless excitements, disappointments and despairs, the lists of her successes and reasons for happiness rehearsed in letters to parents and grandparents, recall the young Sylvia Plath. I read the childhood poems first, but soon turned to the end of the book to read backwards, to find out if she had become a real writer.

No, this is not a rare precocious writing talent, but the book is more than readable, and proceeds will help fund music and drama training for young people. Anthologists who collect thematically for educational material should read Sophie's Log for extracts of prose or for poems, especially "Sunglasses", "On being alone at a Railway Station", and the childhood poem, "Swans on the Wing".

The End.....
or is it the beginning?